The Algebra Journal

ISBN: 978-1-4357-5314-3

THE ALGEBRA

(al-jabr)

Journal

Solving The Mysteries of The UNKNOWN

Numbers

The number concept began with God; He initiated numbers back in the beginning.

Genesis 1 tells us about the creation of the world in seven days, counting them out and delineating the events of each one.

Genesis 1:10-14 describes a river in Eden which is divided into four branches. Here is the concept of a whole and parts.

The various genealogies show the keeping of records of time and the counting of years.

Everywhere in Scripture number concepts are used!

PARADISI IN SOLE
Paradisus Terrestris

The Garden
of Eden

Copied from an
old engraving.

3

THE SEVEN DAYS OF CREATION

DAY 7 SABAT REST
DAY 6 ANIMALS & MAN
DAY 2 SKY & WATER
DAY 3 LAND SEA VEGETATION
IN THE BEGINNING
DAY 1 THE LIGHT
DAY 5 FISH & BIRDS
DAY 4 SUN, MOON, STARS

Exemplify
sequence
pattern
order

THE FOUR OPERATIONS OF MATHEMATICS

ADDING & SUBTRACTING
MULTIPLYING & DIVIDING
PARENTHESES
COUNTING
EXPONENTS & ROOTS

This also has sequence,
pattern and order.

The seven days of creation
exemplify sequence and pattern.

Sequence and pattern are firmly
established and may not be modified.

The sequence & pattern in math
is also firmly established.

Math is learned in the following
order or sequence:

1- Counting
2- Adding & Subtracting
3- Multiplying & Dividing
4- Exponents

The order in which we apply these
operations to expressions is the
reverse - after parentheses -

1- Exponents
2- Multiplying & Dividing
3- Adding & Subtracting.

Like unwinding the coil, you must begin
at the end.

NUMBER/COUNTING SYSTEMS

BABYLONIAN (1500 B.C.)

1	2	3	4	5	6	7	8	9	10
▼	▼▼	▼▼▼	▼▼▼▼	▼▼▼ ▼▼	▼▼▼ ▼▼▼	▼▼▼ ▼▼▼ ▼	▼▼▼ ▼▼▼ ▼▼	▼▼▼ ▼▼▼ ▼▼▼	◄

CHINESE (500 B.C.)

1	2	3	4	5	6	7	8	9	10
一	二	三	四	五	六	七	八	九	十

EGYPTIAN (300 B.C.)

1	2	3	4	5	6	7	8	9	10
I	II	III	IIII	III II	III III	IIII III	IIII IIII	IIII III II	∩ Cow's Hoof

100	1,000	10,000	100,000	1,000,000
◎	𓆸	👆	🐸	𓀀
Coiled Rope	Flower	Finger	Frog	God

12,425 birds

GREEK (400 B.C.)

1	2	3	4	5	6	7	8	9	10
A	B	Γ	Δ	E	F	Z	H	θ	I

ROMAN (200 B.C.)

1	2	3	4	5	6	7	8	9	10
I	II	III	IV	V	VI	VII	VIII	IX	X

50	100	1000	500
L	C	M	D

The Bible says that —
God gave man the mathematical dimensions. Man built it.

width
50
Cubits

TOP VIEW

Length = 300 Cubits

A cubit ranged in length from 18–22 inches

height
30
Cubits

↑ 3 height add man!

(The ark was quite large.)

NOAH'S ARK
{ The description and dimensions can be found in Genesis 6:14–16 }

The first example in the Bible of Math being used to build something.

↗

Some Calculations of the size of the ark.

A cubit was the measure of a man's forearm from elbow to finger tip

←— 1 cubit —→

If we assume that a cubit equals 18 inches, then the ark would have been 450 ft. long, 75 feet wide, and 45 feet in height.

The RATIO of length to width $\frac{450}{75} = \frac{6}{1}$ would have given it excellent stability - almost impossible to tip over. Josephus says it was cross-braced.

It had 3 decks - so the total available floor space would have been over 100,000 sq. ft. Possibly there were 4 decks (Josephus)

The total cubic volume would have been 1,518,000 cubic feet. - equal to the capacity of 569 modern railroad stock cars.

Space for animals in the ARK

No more than 35,000 animals needed to go on the ark. We can exclude all the animals that could have survived outside the ark such as fish, aquatic animals, amphibians, some reptiles, and insects.

There would have been only a relative few large animals. Most animals would have been small animals such as rabbits, rodents, canines, felines, etc.

If the average size of the animals was roughly the size of a sheep, the ark could have easily carried 50,000 animals with room to spare!

The average stock car (double decker) can accomodate 240 sheep.

$$569 = \text{Cars (equivalent volume)}$$
$$\times \ \ 240 = \text{sheep per car}$$
$$136,560 = \text{Sheep that could have fit into the ark.}$$

9

HEBREW NUMBERS

LETTERS HAVE NUMERICAL VALUE. THE
LETTERS ALEF THROUGH YOD ARE USED FOR
THE NUMBERS 1-10.

100 ק	10 י yod	1 א Alef	
200 ר	20 ך,כ	2 ב Samech	
300 ש	30 ל	3 ג Nun	
400 ת	40 ם,מ	4 ד Nun	
	50 ן,נ	5 ה Mem	
	60 ס	6 ו Mem	
	70 ע	7 ז Lamed	
	80 ף,פ	8 ח Khaf	
	90 ץ,צ	9 ט Kaf	

Hebrew is written right to left. When
combining characters, it makes no difference
what order they are placed in.

Some Observations about Noah's Ark

1 - The design of the ark involved
   exact mathematical calculations.

2 - The math for the design was given
   to Noah (a mathematician) by God.
   It was divinely inspired.

3 - Noah used the math to build
   the ark which saved his family
   and the animals from the flood.

4 - Math provided the "key" to
   their safety.

5 - Noah and his sons actually had
   to do the work.

6 - Math today gives us "keys"
   but we have to do the actual work.

The Account of The building of the Tower of Babel

This is the second example in the Bible of math being used to construct something. Although the math is not mentioned in the scriptures, it is obvious, if a building the size of the tower of Babel is constructed, a great deal of math would be involved. Unlike the ark, the tower is an example of the misuse of math.

The Babylonian name for the tower is "ETEMENANKI"

In 460 B.C. Herodotus wrote of a tower, "It has a solid central tower, one furlong square, with a second erected on top of it and then a third and so on up to eight. All eight towers can be climbed by a spiral way running around the outside."

The Tower of Babel

Construction of the tower would have
required extensive knowledge of
Math and construction.

13

Observations on the building of
The Tower of Babel

1 - This is an example of the misuse of math because the purpose of the tower was to reach to the heavens.

It was man's attempt to become equal to God through his own wisdom and strength.

2 - Math is a powerful tool that may be used for good or evil.

3 - We should avoid a prideful attitude or an attitude of greed or lustful power

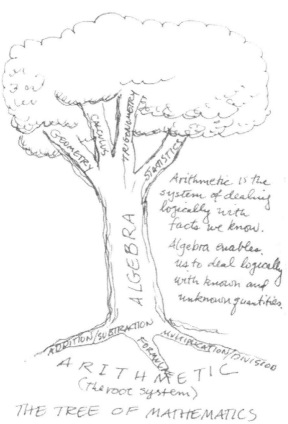

Arithmetic is the system of dealing logically with facts we know.

Algebra enables us to deal logically with known and unknown quantities.

GEOMETRY
CALCULUS
TRIGONOMETRY
STATISTICS
ALGEBRA
ADDITION / SUBTRACTION
FORMULAE
MULTIPLICATION / DIVISION

A R I T H M E T I C
(the root system)

THE TREE OF MATHEMATICS

ALGEBRA IS THE
TRUNK OF THE TREE

15

The Keys to Logical Procedures
in Algebra
(The Properties)

 IDENTITY

<u>ADDITIVE</u>: For any number a,
$$a + 0 = a$$
You can add zero to
any number w/o changing its identity

<u>MULTIPLICATIVE</u>: For any number a,
$$a \cdot 1 = a$$
You can multiply by one w/o changing its identity
-- on the other hand ---

<u>MULTIPLICATIVE PROPERTY OF ZERO</u>
$$a \cdot 0 = 0 \quad \text{(Remember division by zero is not allowed)}$$

 EQUALITY

<u>REFLEXIVE</u>
$$a = a$$

<u>SYMMETRIC</u>
If $a = b$ then $b = a$

<u>TRANSITIVE</u>
If $a = b$ and $b = c$ then $a = c$

<u>SUBSTITUTION</u>
If $a = b$, then a may be replaced by b.

 **COMMUTATIVE** · For any numbers a and b,

$$a + b = b + a$$

and

$$a \cdot b = b \cdot a$$

You may add or multiply in any order.

 **ASSOCIATIVE** For any numbers a, b, and c (where there are 3 or more)

$$(a + b) + c = a + (b + c)$$

and

$$(ab)c = a(bc)$$

You may add or multiply in any combinations.
This applies to GROUPING of elements.

DISTRIBUTIVE Officially called: "THE DISTRIBUTIVE LAW OF MULTIPLICATION OVER ADDITION"

For any numbers a, b, and c (more than 2)

$$a(b+c) = ab + ac \quad \text{and} \quad (b+c)a = ba + ca$$

$$a(b-c) = ab - ac \quad \text{and} \quad (b-c)a = ba - ca$$

You must multiply <u>each element</u> in the addition/subtraction part of the expression.

17

These "keys" which have also been called "properties" and "Laws" form the basis for all algebraic procedures.

If we think of algebra as a game, these are the "moves".

The challenge is to learn how to employ these basic moves to arrive at complex solutions.

That is where imagination and inventiveness play an important role – something which does not exist in arithmetic where the emphasis is upon mastery of mechanics.

The oldest surviving manuscript
on mathematics, including algebra, is
the Rhind papyrus, written about 1650 B.C.
by the scribe Ahmes and named after
the Englishman who purchased it in 1858.
The papyrus is a scroll 0.5 × 5.5 meters,
and is written in hieratic which was
a cursive form of hieroglyphics.

(Egyptian)

Seated Scribe, limestone 2700-2200 B.C.

The Rhind (or Ahmes)
papyrus
contains 84
mathematical problems

Ahmes states in the papyrus that he is copying a scroll that was 200 years older.

The scroll tells us some interesting things about Egyptian math:

A) Egyptians used unit fractions - fractions with 1 as the numerator. To represent $\frac{2}{7}$, they used $\frac{2}{7} = \frac{1}{4} + \frac{1}{28}$

B) Multiplication was done by using a doubling table and adding. For example, to find 5×3 first double

$1 \times 3 = 3$
$2 \times 3 = 6$ then add $= 15$
$4 \times 3 = 12$

The Rhind papyrus had examples of geometry problems, fractions, and miscellaneous problems including algebra.

22

"Accurate reckoning – the entrance into knowledge of all existing things and all obscure secrets." – Ahmes

Ahmes' Problem

Divide 100 loaves among 10 men so that 3 of the men receive double portions.

Ahmes had no symbol for zero. Minus (negative) numbers were not used. His algebra was "rhetorical" because only words and numbers were used. There were no symbols for unknown variables.

23

The Rhind papyrus gives us examples and tables.

the Rhind papyrus is not a mathematical treatise. It leaves many things unexplained. It is still a mystery what system the Egyptians used to derive the tables of unit fractions.

The Egyptian priests knew that there was power in a knowledge of mathematics. For that reason, they were interested in keeping the knowledge a secret from all the uninitiated.

Number systems which do not
have a zero or minus numbers
are severely limited.

If we were only concerned about
constructing / building tangible
Objects, the need for zero and minus
numbers may not be so obvious.

However, we need numbers for

ACCOUNTING - which show profit (+)
            and loss (-)

TEMPERATURE - Above zero, zero, and
                below zero temperatures.

VELOCITY IN A CERTAIN DIRECTION - we
            need numbers to represent
              movement in the opposite
Increase and decrease   direction.

THE NUMBER LINE (a concept)

What we refer to as "the number line" is
represented thus —

Using 2 strips, we can demonstrate
addition and subtraction:

For addition, place the zero of the second strip under
the number on the 1st strip for the first addend.
In this example, the zero is placed under
the 2 on the top strip.

Now read the second addend on the lower strip.
The sum will be the number directly above
on the top strip.

Experimentation will show all the
possibilities of addition and subtraction

To subtract, place the first number on the top strip directly above the second number on the lower strip. The answer is the number on the top strip directly above the zero on the bottom strip.

Example: 7 - 2

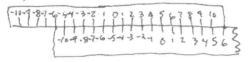

5, which is the correct answer is directly above the zero.

Now, if we add a positive and a negative number we can see -

4 + (-3)

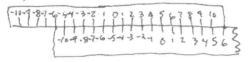

The answer is 1

Subtracting a positive and negative number

4 - (-3)   The answer is 7

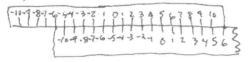

Addition and subtraction can
be represented one dimensionally
with 2 strips (number lines).
Multiplication and division require
a 2-dimensional diagram.

MULTIPLICATION OF POSITIVE AND NEGATIVE NUMBERS

	4	3	2	1	0	-1	-2	-3	-4
4	16	12	8	4	0	-4	-8	-12	-16
3	12	9	6	3	0	-3	-6	-9	-12
2	8	6	4	2	0	-2	-4	-6	-8
1	4	3	2	1	0	-1	-2	-3	-4
0	0	0	0	0	0	0	0	0	0
-1	-4	-3	-2	-1	0	1	2	3	4
-2	-8	-6	-4	-2	0	2	4	6	8
-3	-12	-9	-6	-3	0	3	6	9	12
-4	-16	-12	-8	-4	0	4	8	12	16

Blue = positive   Red = negative   Yellow = zero

TABLES OF RELATIONSHIPS

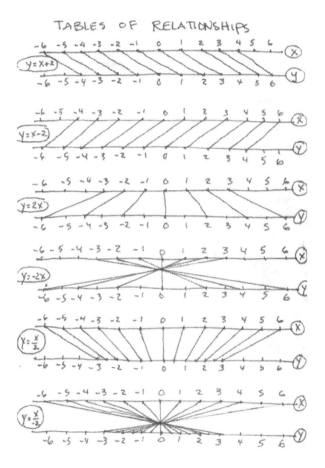

The rules for integers apply to rational numbers.

ADDITION: If 2 rational numbers have the same sign, add their absolute values and give the sum the same sign as the addends.

If they have different signs, subtract the lesser absolute value from the larger and give the difference the sign of the addend with the greater absolute value.

SUBTRACTION: To subtract a number, add its additive inverse. The rules for addition apply.

MULTIPLICATION : The product of 2
numbers which have the same sign
(pos or neg) is positive
The product of 2 numbers having
different signs is negative.

DIVISION : The same as for
multiplication because
division is actually multiplication
by the multiplicative inverse of
the number that is the divisor.

Mistakes with minus signs are
the most common in algebra.

32

Διοφαντυσ

Diophantus

Diophantus was a Greek mathematician who worked in Alexandria around 250 AD. Called by some "The Father of Algebra", he wrote a 13 volume treatise on math of which we have 6 volumes. The other seven volumes have been lost.

Diophantus was the first that we know of who used letters for variables — developing the <u>syncopated</u> style of writing equations.

$$\varsigma \iota \sigma \beta \qquad x = 2$$
$$\varsigma \gamma \iota \sigma \theta \qquad x + 3 = 9$$
$$\varsigma \gamma \beta \iota \sigma \theta \qquad 3x + 2 = 9$$

Diophantus's equations continued---

$$ςθΛγιοβ \qquad 9X - 3 = 2$$

$$ςβΛθιοςγ \qquad 2X - 9 = X + 3$$

$$ςβθιοςΔγ \qquad 2X + 9 = X - 3$$

Diophantus made numerous contributions in the area of algebraic symbolism.

However, he only worked with integers. Consequently, a Diophantine equation involves only integers as coefficients.

The Greeks handled irrational numbers with geometric models.

Algebra as Math / Algebra as Language

Rhetorical statements can be translated into algebraic expressions and equations. (Using symbolic representation)

ADD	SUBTRACT
SUM OF	THE DIFFERENCE
TOTAL OF	FEWER
PLUS	LESS
INCREASE	REDUCE BY
MORE	DECREASE BY

MULTIPLY	DIVIDE
OF	RATIO
TIMES	QUOTIENT
PRODUCT	PER
FACTORS OF	AVERAGE

These are some of the most commonly used terms.

Being able to translate words into algebraic symbols is critical.

35

Work with numbers (knowns) and letters (unknowns) to form sentences (expressions & equations) that can be solved.

Use + to represent addition.

Use − to represent subtraction

Use no symbol for multiplication. Instead write elements together such as 2x which mean 2 times x.

You can also use parenthesis to show multiplication 2(x + y). (the dot may be used when necessary)

Use the — symbol for division.

Note: the ÷ symbol probably comes from

$$\frac{2}{4} = 2 \div 4$$

TRANSLATION PROBLEM

Often words do not make clear
how to group terms. You have to
figure it out by context. Group things
the only way it makes sense. Using
parentheses can help.

A TRANSLATION FORMULA:
(That only works when the appropriate
words are used.)

$$\text{The}\begin{Bmatrix}\text{SUM}\\\text{DIFFERENCE}\\\text{PRODUCT}\\\text{QUOTIENT}\end{Bmatrix}\text{OF (between)}\quad a \text{ and } B \text{ is } a \overset{+}{\underset{\times}{-}} b$$

The problem is that there are many
and varied ways the language
uses to express these things.
Example, 5 less than X is X - 5

TRANSLATING:

ANSWER 2 QUESTIONS

① How are the terms grouped?

② What are the operations (relationships) among the groups?

TWO OBSERVATIONS

① Rhetorical statements cannot be translated word for word.

② Complicated things can be written in algebraic notation that are difficult to write about in words, because the verbal expressions can get very complicated and it can be difficult to tell where the grouping is.

THE ACCURATE TRANSLATION OF CONCEPTS (OFTEN EXPRESSED IN WORDS) INTO ALGEBRAIC NOTATION IS THE FIRST BIG STEP FOR THE STUDENT OF ALGEBRA.

MOVING FROM THE CLOUD TO THE SOLID STRUCTURE

CONCEPT
(THE CLOUD)

Step 1   Step 2
ANALYZE   ANALYZE

OPERATIONS
(STRUCTURE)

GROUP
(FOUNDATION)

To move
from
concept to
expression

The groups identify what it
is that you have to work with.
If this is not done correctly, every-
thing that follows will be incorrect.

DIOPHANTUS

DIOPHANTUS PASSED ONE SIXTH OF HIS LIFE IN CHILDHOOD, ONE TWELFTH IN YOUTH, AND ONE SEVENTH MORE AS A BACHELOR. FIVE YEARS AFTER HIS MARRIAGE, THERE WAS BORN A SON WHO DIED FOUR YEARS BEFORE HIS FATHER, AT HALF HIS FATHER'S FINAL AGE. HOW OLD WAS DIOPHANTUS WHEN HE DIED?

(the Diophantus epitaph problem)

This strange engraving is on the title
page of the latin translation of Diophantus's
"ARITHMETICA"

perhaps the message is that math relates to nature
and music.

41

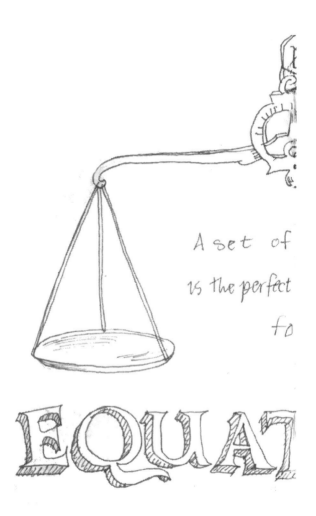

A set of

is the perfect

to

EQUAT

scales

illustration

r

TIONS

Solving equations is what algebra is all about.

The Rule for solving equations: whatever you do to one side of the equation, you must also do to the other side.

We may add, subtract, multiply, divide both sides of the equation

---

The goal (the solution) is to convert the equation into its simplest form.

unknown = known

Solving equations is
unraveling the mystery of the
unknown.

SOLVE BY ADDITION

$$y - 8 = 13$$
$$+8 \quad +8 \quad \leftarrow \text{ add } 8$$
$+8$ ⌐ $y = 21$

SOLVE BY SUBTRACTION

$$x + 15 = -6$$
$$-15 \quad -15 \quad \leftarrow \text{ subtract } 15$$
-15 ⌐ $x = -21$

SOLVE BY MULTIPLICATION

$$24 \cdot \frac{x}{24} = \frac{5}{12} \cdot 24$$
$$\leftarrow \text{ multiply by } 24$$
$\cdot 24$ ⌐ $x = 10$

SOLVE BY DIVISION

$$\frac{-6x}{-6} = \frac{11}{-6}$$
$$\leftarrow \text{ divide by } -6$$
$\div -6$ ⌐ $x = -\frac{11}{6}$

SIMPLE EQUATIONS CAN BE REPRESENTED CONCRETELY

POSITIVE NUMBERS = (+)

NEGATIVE NUMBERS = (−)

VARIABLES = ⛷ (A CUP · TO HOLD ANY QUANTITY)

EXAMPLES:

$$X + 3 = 5$$

⛷ (+)(+)(+) = (+)(+)(+)(+)(+)

SUBTRACT 3 (ADD −3)

⛷ = (+)(+)

$$X = 2$$

$$2x + 3 = 11$$

ADD -1

DIVIDE

$$x = 4$$

Most of the time equations
involve more than one
operation as above.

$$4x - 7 = 5$$
$$ + 7 \quad +7$$

$+7 \Big|$ $\quad \dfrac{4x}{4} = \dfrac{12}{4}$ $\qquad$ (2 STEPS)

$\div 4 \Big|$ $\qquad x = 3$

$-\cancel{6}\dfrac{(-3n - (-4))}{-6} = -9 \cdot -6$

$-6 \Big|$ $\quad -3n - (-4) = +54$ $\qquad$ ①

$\begin{array}{c}\text{COMBINE} \\ \text{SIMPLIFY}\end{array} \Big|$ $-3n + 4 = 54$ $\qquad$ ②
$$ -4 \quad -4$$

$-4 \Big|$ $\quad \dfrac{-3n}{-3} = \dfrac{50}{-3}$ $\qquad$ ③

$\div -3 \Big|$ $\qquad n = -\dfrac{50}{3}$ $\qquad$ ④

4 STEPS TO
UNRAVELING THE
MYSTERY OF
48 $\qquad$ THE UNKNOWN

GENERALLY, YOU CAN

1. LOOK FOR WAYS to SIMPLIFY (REMOVE PARENTHESIS OR DENOMINATORS)

2. SEE WHAT YOU CAN ADD OR SUBTRACT

3. SEE IF YOU NEED TO MULTIPLY OF DIVIDE.

EXAMPLE:

$$2(x-1) = 3(x-2)$$

SIMPLIFY $\Big|$ $2x - 2 = 3x - 6$

$-3x$ $\qquad$ $-3x$

$-3x \Big|$ $-x - 2 = -6$

$\qquad$ $+2 \qquad +2$

$+2 \Big|$ $-x = -4$

$-1 \Big|$ $x = 4$

49

THE STEP METHOD

EQUATION

OPERATION	RESULT
OPERATION	RESULT

$$3 \cdot \frac{X}{3} \quad \frac{3}{1} 2(X-1) = \frac{4}{1} \cdot 3$$

$$\cdot 3 \quad | \quad X - 6(X-1) = 12$$

SIMPLIFY $\quad | \quad X - 6X + 6 = 12$

COMBINE $\quad | \quad -5X + 6 = 12$
$$\qquad\qquad\qquad -6 \quad -6$$

$-6 \quad | \quad \dfrac{-5X}{-5} = \dfrac{6}{-5}$

$\div -5 \quad | \quad X = -\dfrac{6}{5}$

50.

"ALGEBRA"

IN approximately 825 A.D.,
AL-Khowarizmi, an Arab
mathematician wrote a treatise
on equations titled "Hisāb al-jabr
W'al-muqābala" which meant "the
Calculation of reduction and
restoration." It was translated into
Latin in 1140 A.D. The translation
was titled "Liber algebrae et almucabala".
This is where we get the word, algebra.

AL-Khwarizmi

SOLVING EQUATIONS

INVOLVES

① SKILL IN HANDLING
ALGEBRAIC EXPRESSIONS

AND

② INSIGHTFUL ANALYSIS
(IMAGINATION)
TO FIGURE OUT A
STRATEGY THAT
WILL WORK
SUCCESSFULLY.

SKILL + IMAGINATION

MORE ON HANDLING EXPRESSIONS USING THE DISTRIBUTIVE PROPERTY.

$$3(x+4)$$

USE 'TILES'
TO SHOW HOW
THE DISTRIBUTIVE
PROPERTY WORKS

STEP 1: MARK OFF
$$3 \cdot (x+4)$$
USE TILES TO
MEASURE

STEP 2: FILL IN WITH LINES
THEN TILES

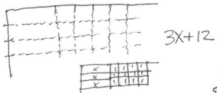

$$3x+12$$

53

IS $3(x+3) =$ OR $\neq$ $3x+3$?

BUILD

$x+3$

3 ... $= 3x+9$

$\therefore 3(x+3) \neq 3x+3$

$10(x+3)$
$10 \cdot x + 10 \cdot 3$
$10x+30$

USING THE DISTRIBUTIVE PROPERTY, WE KNOW THAT THE MULTIPLICATION BY 10 IS DISTRIBUTED OVER BOTH TERMS IN PARENTHESIS

USING COUNTERS

NOTE: 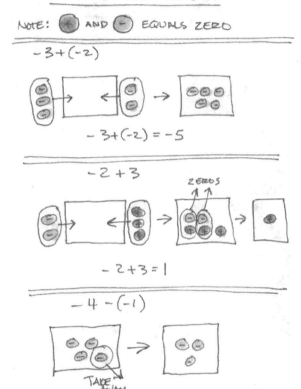 AND ⬤ EQUALS ZERO

$-3 + (-2)$

$-3 + (-2) = -5$

$-2 + 3$

ZEROS

$-2 + 3 = 1$

$-4 - (-1)$

TAKE AWAY

$-4 - (-1) = \not{3} - 3$

$$3 - (-2)$$

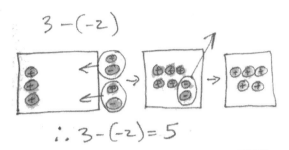

$$\therefore 3 - (-2) = 5$$

PROPERTIES OF EQUALITY

 **ADDITION**

If $a = b$
Then $a + c = b + c$

 **SUBTRACTION**

If $a = b$
Then $a - c = b - c$

MULTIPLICATION

If $a = b$
Then $a \cdot c = b \cdot c$

DIVISION

If $a = b$
Then $\dfrac{a}{c} = \dfrac{b}{c}$ where $c \neq 0$

56

3(4) means 3 groups of 4

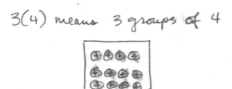

3(-4) means 3 groups of -4

-3(4) means remove 3 groups
of 4. To do this, place
zero pairs first.

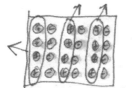
-12
is left

-3(-4) means remove 3 groups
of -4 from the same set up.
That will leave +12 .

Using models to solve equations:

$$2x + 2 = -4$$

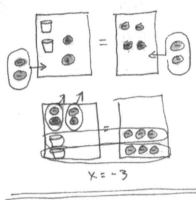

$$x = -3$$

$$w - 3 = 2w - 1$$

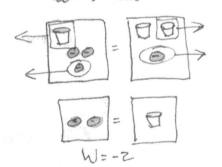

$$w = -2$$

PERIMETER - AREA EQUATIONS

PERIMETER = 148 INCHES
LENGTH = 3X + 17
WIDTH = X

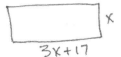

$$3X + 17$$

$$2X + 2(3X+17) = 148$$

SIMP. $\quad 2X + 6X + 34 = 148$

COMB. $\quad 8X + 34 = 148$
$$ -34 \qquad -34$$

-34 $\quad \dfrac{8X}{8} = \dfrac{114}{8}$

$\div 8$ $\quad X = 14\frac{1}{4}$

WIDTH = $14\frac{1}{4}$
LENGTH = $59\frac{3}{4}$

2 SPECIAL CASES
EQUATIONS WITH NO SOLUTIONS

Some equations have no
solutions because there is
insufficient data to set up
a true equation.

EXAMPLE:

$$2x + 5 = 2x - 3$$
$$-2x \qquad -2x$$
$$-2x \mid 5 = -3$$

Since $5 = -3$ is a false
statement, this equation
is not true and cannot
be solved.

UNTRUE EQUATIONS
CANNOT BE SOLVED

SOME EQUATIONS MAY
HAVE EVERY NUMBER IN
THE SOLUTION SETS. AN
EQUATION THAT IS TRUE
FOR EVERY VALUE IS
CALLED AN <u>IDENTITY</u>.

EXAMPLE:

$$3(x+1) - 5 = 3x - 2$$

SIMP $\overline{3x + 3 - 5 = 3x - 2}$

COMB $\overline{3x - 2 = 3x - 2}$

Since the expressions on
both sides of the equation are
the same, this equation is
an identity.

61

MORE PERIMETER / AREA EQUATIONS

$P = 23$
$A = 30$

X [rectangle, width labeled $11.5 - X$]

H · B $= A$

$X(11.5 - X) = 30$

$11.5X - X^2 = 30$

$-X^2 + 11.5X - 30 = 0$

$X^2 - 11.5X + 30 = 0$

IS A

QUADRATIC EQUATION

If we incorporate area, we have to deal with squared values which are quadratic.

Someone said that

Algebra is arithmetic backwards.
The reason is evident when
you compare the kinds of
problems involving perimeter.

ARITHMETIC

The height of a rectangle is
7 inches. The width is 13 inches.
What is the perimeter.

$$2(7 + 13) = 40$$

ALGEBRA

The perimeter of a rectangle
is 40. The width is 6 inches
longer than the height. What are
the height and width?

$$x + x + 6 = 20 \rightarrow 2x = 14$$
$$x = 7$$

APPLICATIONS

Algebra can be used in real situations.

$ __Sales__: Karen has 6 more than twice as many newspapers customers as when she started selling newspapers. She now has 98 customers. How many did she have when she started?

x = original customers

Let $2x + 6$ equal the number of customers now

$$2x + 6 = 98$$

-6 $\quad 2x = 92$

$\div 2$ $\quad \dfrac{2x}{2} = \dfrac{92}{2}$

$\qquad x = 46$

Sports: One season, a baseball player scored 9 more than twice the number of runs he batted in. He scored 117 runs that season. How many runs did he bat in?

Let x = runs batted in

$2x + 9$ = runs scored

$$2x + 9 = 117$$
$$-9 \quad -9$$

$-9 \mid$

$$2x = 108$$
$$\frac{2x}{2} = \frac{108}{2}$$

$\div 2 \mid$

$$x = 54$$

Statistics: A student has an average of 76 on four tests. What score does he have to get on the 100-point final test if it counts double and he wants to have an average of 80 or better? Is it possible for him to have an average of 85?

Let X = grade on final test

$$\frac{\overset{\text{tests}}{4}(\overset{\text{AVG.}}{76}) + \overset{\text{COUNTS DBL.}}{2X}}{\underset{\uparrow \text{test scores (4+2)}}{6}} = 80 \quad \text{if } x = 100$$

$\times 6$ | $4(76) + 2X = 480$

$304 \quad -304$

-304 | $2X = 176$

$\div 2$ | $X = 88$

$304 + 200 \lessgtr 6 \cdot 85$

$504 < 510$

$88, \text{ NO}$

TRAVEL: An employee drove to work at 40 MPH and arrived 1 minute late. She left home at the same time the next day and averaged 45 MPH and arrived one minute early. How far does she drive to work?

Use rate · time = distance

Let $x = \dfrac{\text{base}}{\text{time}}$ in minutes

$$(40 \cdot 60)(x + 1) = (45 \cdot 60)(x - 1)$$

simp | $2400x + 2400 = 2700x - 2700$
$-2400 -2400$

−2400 | $2400x = 2700x - 5100$
$-2700x -2700x$

−2700x | $\dfrac{-300x}{-300} = \dfrac{-5100}{-300}$

÷ −300 | $x = 17$

$17 + 1 = \dfrac{18}{60} \cdot 40 = 12 \text{ miles}$

construction: A rectangular playground is 60 meters longer than it is wide. It is enclosed by 920 meters of fencing. Find its length.

for $X = $ length

Then width $= X - 60$

$$2(X + X - 60) = 920$$

Simp. $\overline{\smash{\big)}\,4X - 120 = 920}$

$\quad +120 \qquad +120$

$+120 \,\overline{\smash{\big)}\,4X = 1040}$

$\div 4 \,\overline{\smash{\big)}\,X = 260}$

260 meters is the length.

NUMBER
CLASSIFICATIONS

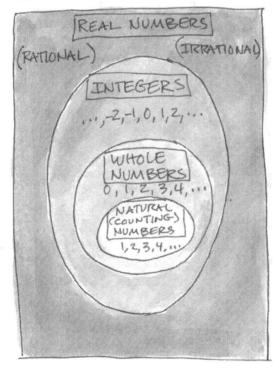

REAL NUMBERS

(RATIONAL)   (IRRATIONAL)

INTEGERS

..., -2, -1, 0, 1, 2, ...

WHOLE
NUMBERS
0, 1, 2, 3, 4, ...

NATURAL
(COUNTING)
NUMBERS
1, 2, 3, 4, ...

MAGIC SQUARES

How to construct a 3 X 3 Square.

1. FIRST

1	2	3
4	5	6
7	8	9

2. ROTATE

3. SWITCH CORNER NUMBERS

4. REARRANGE
SO THE DIAMOND BECOMES
A SQUARE
THUS:

$$2 \ 7 \ 6$$
$$9 \ 5 \ 1$$
$$4 \ 3 \ 8$$

An example of number sets.

2	7	6
9	5	1
4	3	8

ADDS UP TO
15 EVERY
DIRECTION

IF WE SUBTRACT 5 FROM EACH
NUMBER —

$$-3 \ \ 2 \ \ 1$$
$$4 \ \ 0 \ -4$$
$$-1 \ -2 \ \ 3$$

ADDS UP TO ZERO EACH WAY!

70

Equations involving
consecutive numbers

1. Let x = the smallest number

2. Let x + difference = other numbers in the sequence

Example #1   3 consecutive numbers total 27

Let x = smallest
$$x+1 = \text{next number} (1^{st} + \text{Diff})$$
$$x+2 = \text{next number} (1^{st} + \text{Diff})$$

So $x + x+1 + x+2 = 27$

Combine $3x + 3 = 27$
    -3 $-3 \quad -3$
    $\div 3$ $\dfrac{3x = 24}{3 \quad\quad 3}$
                $x = 8$

numbers are
8, 9, 10

Example #2   3 consecutive even numbers total 12

$$x + x+2 + x+4 = 12$$
$$3x = 6$$
$$x = 2$$

numbers are 2, 4, 6

MAZES

There is a particular kind
of maze or labyrinth which
is not a puzzle but requires
the person to trace over every
path in order to reach the goal.

One of the earliest examples
is called the Cretan maze.

You must
cover all
the steps
to get to
the goal

enter
↓

These mazes
appear to be
a visual analogy
to following
the path of
life

Level sequence = 0 3 2 1 4 7 6 5 8

The Hebrew "Jericho" Maze
Ancient Design

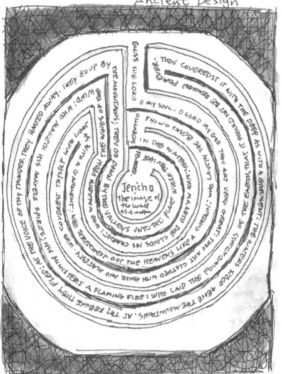

Psalm 104: 1–18, 20, 21 are written on the path.
In the center: "Jericho, The image of the Wall of Jericho.
The reader is as if walking.

A Shortcut for solving equations

In solving the following:

$X + 2 = 4$ subtract 2 from both sides

$X - 2 = 4$ add 2 to both sides

$2X = 4$ divide 2 into both sides

$\frac{X}{2} = 4$ multiply 2 times both sides

The result of these actions is the same as the following:

$X + 2 = 4$ move the +2 to the other side and you subtract

$X - 2 = 4$ move the -2 to the other side and you add

$2X = 4$ move the 2 and mult. changes to division

$\frac{X}{2} = 4$ move the 2 and division becomes multiplication

Shortcut Rule: when a number is moved to the other side, it takes the opposite operation.

74   ✳ BE CAREFUL WITH MULT. AND DIVISION.

| RATIO | $\dfrac{n_1}{n_2}$ | one number n_1 compared to another n_2 |

| PROPORTION | $\dfrac{n_1}{n_2} = \dfrac{n_3}{n_4}$ | 2 ratios equal to each other |

LAW OF PROPORTIONS

THE PRODUCT OF THE MEANS IS EQUAL
to THE PRODUCT OF THE EXTREMES

$$OR \quad n_1 \cdot n_4 = n_2 \cdot n_3$$

Proportions are one of the
most frequently used
constructions in algebra.
They are also frequently
used in real world situations.

SETTING UP VARIOUS KINDS OF EQUATIONS

Ratios and proportions are just one kind of typical equation.

PERCENT
(a kind of ratio)

$$\frac{PART}{WHOLE} = \frac{\%}{100}$$

SIMPLE INTEREST

Uses the formula:

$$\underline{Interest = Deposit \cdot rate \cdot time\,(annual)}$$

$$Interest = Dollars \cdot \frac{\%}{time} \cdot time$$

PERCENT OF CHANGE

a kind of percent

$$\frac{\text{AMOUNT OF CHANGE}}{\text{BASE (ORIGINAL)}} = \frac{\%}{100}$$

MIXTURES

these involve a combination of 2 or more parts into a whole. You are supposed to find information about one or more of the parts when information about the whole is given.

Often mixtures involve calculating an average.

MOTION

Use the formula

Distance = Rate · time

Miles = miles/HR · n hours = n Miles

Direct Variation Problems

$$y = kx$$

One variable = Constant · another variable

to find the constant use:

$$k = \frac{y}{x}$$

Inverse Variation

$$xy = k$$

As one variable increases, the other decreases. Hence, it's called an inverse variation.

Examples:

① Twenty fish were captured, tagged, and returned. Later, 29 fish were caught. Of these 3 had tags. Estimate the number of fish in the body of water.

IDENTIFY: This is a proportion problem

SET UP: Let x = total number of fish

$$\frac{20}{x} = \frac{3}{29}$$

SOLVE

CROSS
x X $\quad$ $20 \times 29 = 3x$ $\qquad$ $\begin{array}{r} \overset{1}{2}9 \\ 26 \\ \hline 580 \end{array}$

$\quad$ $3x = 580$

$\quad$ $x = \frac{580}{3}$ $\quad$ $x = 193$ (rounded)

The answer is rounded because you can't have $\frac{1}{7}$ of a fish.

② 50 is what percent of 60

IDENTIFY: This is a percent problem

SET UP: $\dfrac{PART}{WHOLE} = \dfrac{\%}{100}$ Let X = %

SOLVE

$$\dfrac{50}{60} = \dfrac{X}{100}$$

CROSS-
MULT. $5,000 = 60X$ 50 is $83\frac{1}{3}$% of 60

$X = 83\frac{1}{3}$

③ An investor invested $30,000, part at 6% annual interest and the rest at 7.5% annual interest. The earnings were $1995 in interest. How much was invested at each rate?

IDENTIFY: SIMPLE INTEREST PROB.

SET UP: Let X = amount at 6%
        Then 30,000 - X = amount at 7.5%

SOLVE:
$0.06X + 0.075(30000 - X) = 1995$

$- 0.015X = -255$

$X = 17,000$ $17,000 at 6%
              $13,000 at 7.5%

④ A chemistry experiment calls for a 36% solution of copper sulfate. There is a 40 mL of 25% solution. How many milliliters of a 60% solution will need to be added?

IDENTIFY: This is a mixture-percent problem

SET-UP: Set x = amount of 60% solution needed.

$$0.25(40) + 0.60x = 0.30(40+x)$$
$$10 + 0.6x = 12 + 0.3x$$
$$0.3x = 2$$
$$x \approx 6.7 \text{ (Rounded to nearest tenth)}$$

⑤ Two cars travel in opposite directions. One travels at 80 km/hr and the other at 72 km/hr. In how many hours will they be 760 km apart?

IDENTIFY: MOTION PROB. $D = r \cdot t$

SET-UP: $(r \cdot t) + (r \cdot t) = 760$
$$80t + 72t = 760$$
$$152t = 760$$
$$t = 5 \qquad 5 \text{ hours}$$

EXAMPLES (Continued)

⑥ With all his gear on, Neil Armstrong weighed 360 Lbs on earth, but on the moon he weighed only 60 Lbs. A girl weighs 108 Lbs on earth. What would she weigh on the moon?

IDENTIFY: This is a direct variation prob.

SET-UP: $k = \frac{60}{360} = \frac{1}{6}$

Let x = girl's weight on moon

$$\frac{1}{6} = \frac{x}{108}$$

SOLVE

$6x = 108$ girl's weight on

$x = 18$ the moon = 18 Lbs.

⑦ The pitch of a musical tone varies inversely as its wavelength. If one tone has a pitch of 440 vibrations per second and a wavelength of 2.4 ft., find the wavelength of a tone that has a pitch of 660 vibes per second.

IDENTIFY: this is an inverse variation problem.

⑦(continued)

Set up:

$k = $ pitch · wavelength

SOLVE: $k = (440)(2.4) = 1056$

Set $_{WAVE} = X$ $1056 = X \cdot 660$

$X = \frac{1056}{660} = 1.6$ wavelength $= 1.6$ ft.

The way to work with all those
kinds of problems is:

First, identify what kind of
     a problem it is.

Second, set up the problem
      as an algebraic equation
Third, solve the equation.

THE CALENDAR TRICK

— SEPTEMBER —

SUN	MON	TUE	WED	THU	FRI	SAT
						1
2	3	4	5	6	7	8
9	10	11	12	13	14	15
16	17	18	19	20	21	22
23	24	25	26	27	28	29
30						

Have someone select 4 days in the form of a 2×2 square from anywhere on the calendar. Then have them give you the total of the 4 dates. Divide the total by 4 and then subtract 4. That will give you the first number. Add one for the second and 7 and 8 for the third and fourth.

Example

Let's say someone selects 12, 13, 19, and 20 from the calendar on the opposite page. $12 + 13 + 19 + 20 = 64$. $64 \div 4 = 16$ subtract $4 = 12$. 12 is the first number. The others are 13, 19, and 20.

Proof by algebra (how it works)

Let x = lowest number

then 2nd no. = $x + 1$

3rd no. = $x + 7$

4th no. = $x + 8$

equation expression

$$x + x + 1 + x + 7 + x + 8 = TOTAL$$

combine $4x + 16 = TOTAL$

$$4x = TOTAL - 16$$

$$x = \frac{TOTAL}{4} - \frac{16}{4} = \frac{TOTAL}{4} - 4$$

INEQUALITIES

Inequalities behave very much like equations except:

① Inequalities us < > symbols (also ≤ and ≥) instead of =.

② If, in solving an inequality, you multiply or divide by a negative number, < changes to > and > changes to <.

③ Inequalities have answers that are SETS of numbers.

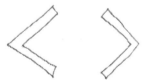

<u>EXAMPLE</u>

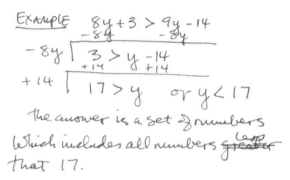

$$8y + 3 > 9y - 14$$
$$\underline{-8y \qquad\qquad -8y}$$

$-8y \mid \quad 3 > y - 14$
$\underline{\qquad\; +14 \qquad +14}$
$+14 \mid \quad 17 > y \qquad$ or $y < 17$

the answer is a set of numbers
which includes all numbers ~~greater~~ less
that 17.

In graphical form:

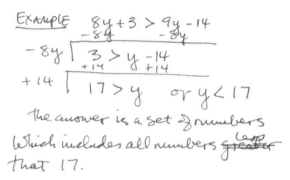

Compound Inequalities

Some compound inequalities such
as $x < 2$ <u>and</u> $x > 4$ have
no numbers in the solution set.
Some compound inequalities use "OR"
and have 2 possibilities for sets

$$x < 2 \quad \underline{OR} \quad x > 4$$

Inequalities lend themselves
to finding solutions to many
real life situations.

EXAMPLE #1

A car gets between 18 and 21 miles per
gallon of gasoline. If the car's gas tank
holds 15 gallons, what is the range of
distance that the car can be driven on one
tank of gasoline?

$$18 \times 15 = 90, \quad 18 \rightarrow 270$$

$$21 \times 15 = 105, \quad 21 \rightarrow 315$$

range = 270 to 315 miles

$$270 \leq R \leq 315.$$

POWERS

— EXPONENTS —

Represented by the small superscripts.

eg. X^2, $(3)^8$, y^7 2, 8, and 7 are exponents.

RULES ⟩

| PRODUCT OF POWERS ⟩ | ADD EXPONENTS $a^n \cdot a^m = a^{n+m}$ |

| POWER OF A POWER ⟩ | MULTIPLY EXPONENTS $(a^n)^m = a^{nm}$ |

| POWER OF A PRODUCT ⟩ | $(Xy)^3 = X^3 y^3$ It is distributive or $(a^m b^n)^p = a^{mp} b^{np}$ |

| QUOTIENT OF POWERS ⟩ | SUBTRACT EXPONENTS $\dfrac{a^m}{a^n} = a^{m-n}$ |

ZERO EXPONENT

ANY QUANTITY TO THE ZERO
POWER EQUALS   1

NEGATIVE EXPONENTS

$$n^{-a} = \frac{1}{n^a}$$

Showing the relationship using a
number line

10^5	10^4	10^3	10^2	10^1	10^0	10^{-1}	10^{-2}	10^{-3}	10^{-4}	10^{-5}
100,000	10,000	1000	100	10	1	$\frac{1}{10}$	$\frac{1}{100}$	$\frac{1}{1000}$	$\frac{1}{10,000}$	$\frac{1}{100,000}$
						.1	.01	.001	.0001	.00001

Exponents give us a convenient system
for handling very large + very small
numbers - "SCIENTIFIC NOTATION" or
        "EXPONENTIAL NOTATION"

90

SUN

◯ MERCURY   DIAMETER
57,900,000 km   5.00 × 10³
from the sun
or 5.79 × 10⁷

◯ VENUS   DIAMETER
              1.208 × 10⁴
108,230,000 km or 1.0823 × 10⁸
DISTANT

◯ EARTH   DIAMETER
              1.276 × 10⁴
149,590,000 DISTANT
              1.4959 × 10⁸

◯ MARS   DIAMETER
         6.79 × 10³ km
227,910,000
         DISTANT 2.2792 × 10⁸

◯ JUPITER DIAMETER 1.432 × 10⁵ km
          DISTANCE 7.78 × 10⁸ km

◯ SATURN DIAMETER 1.21 × 10⁵ km
         DISTANCE 1.427 × 10⁹ km

◯ URANUS DIAMETER 5.18 × 10⁴ km
         DISTANCE 2.87 × 10⁹ km

◯ NEPTUNE DIAMETER 4.95 × 10⁴ km
          DISTANCE 4.497 × 10⁹ km

◯ PLUTO DIAMETER 3 × 10³
        DISTANCE 59 × 10⁹

$6(3)$

3

6 $= 18$

$2(3+2)$

$3+2$

2 $= 10$

$6+4$

1 x x

x x^2

$2(x+1)$ 2 $x+1$ $= 2x+2$

Algebraic expressions can be
classified as:

Monomials $2, a, ab, 2ab^2$ ⎫

binomials 2 monomials ⎬ Polynomials
           eg. $x+y$

trinomials 3 monomials ⎭

etc. $x+y+z$

$X(X+1)$

$\rightarrow$ $= X^2 + X$

$2X(X+2)$

$\rightarrow$ $= 2X^2 + 4X$

AREAS OF RECTANGLES

$= X(2X+1) = 2X^2 + X$

$= 6X^2y^4$

$= 12X^5y^3$

93

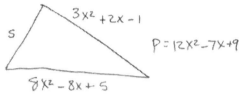

$$12x^2 - 7x + 9 = (3x^2 + 2x - 1) + (8x^2 - 8x + 5) + S$$

SOLVE FOR S

$$\underline{12x^2 - 7x + 9} \quad \underline{-3x^2 - 2x + 1} \quad \underline{-8x^2 + 8x - 5}$$

$$S = (12x^2 - 7x + 9) - (3x^2 + 2x - 1) - (8x^2 - 8x + 5)$$

$$S = x^2 + x + 5 \qquad \text{combining like terms}$$

$$(x + 2)(2x + 3) \qquad \text{MULTIPLYING BINOMIAL}$$

$$= 2x^2 + 7x + 6$$

$$(x + 3)(x + 1)$$

$$= x^2 + 4x + 3$$

THE $\boxed{F}$-$\boxed{O}$-$\boxed{I}$-$\boxed{L}$ METHOD

F   I   R   S   T
O   U   T   S   I   D   E
I   N   S   I   D   E
L   A   S   T

$$\left(\overset{F}{X} + \underset{I}{\overset{L}{2}}\right)\left(\underset{I}{\overset{F}{2}}X + \underset{O}{\overset{L}{1}}\right)$$

The FIRST refers to the 1st monomial in each binomial.

OUTSIDE refers to the terms at either end

INSIDE refers to the terms that are together in the center.

LAST refers to the 2nd term in each binomial

$$\left(\overset{F}{X} + 2\right)\left(2X + \overset{L}{1}\right)$$

$$\underset{2X^2}{\overset{F}{}} + \underset{X}{\overset{O}{}} + \underset{4X}{\overset{I}{}} \underset{+2}{\overset{L}{}}$$

$$2X^2 + 5X + 2$$

95

Demonstrating FOIL By the
Standard multiplication form:

$$X+2$$
$$\times \ 2X+1$$

$$+1X \ +2$$
$$+2X^2+4X$$

$$2X^2+5X \ +2 \qquad \text{Same answer}$$

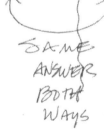

$$(X+2)(2X+1)$$
$$\overset{F}{} \ \overset{O}{} \ \overset{I}{} \ \overset{L}{}$$
$$2X^2 + X + 4X + 2$$

$$2X^2+5X+2$$

$$(2X+1)(X+2)$$
$$\overset{F}{} \ \overset{O}{} \ \overset{I}{} \ \overset{L}{}$$
$$2X^2 +4X + X + 2$$

$$2X^2+5X+2$$

SAME
ANSWER
BOTH
WAYS

FOIL BY 2 FINGERS

FIRST $(2x + 3)(5x + 8) \rightarrow 2x \cdot 5x = 10x^2$

OUTSIDE $(2x + 3)(5x + 8) \rightarrow 2x \cdot 8 = 16x$

INSIDE $(2x + 3)(5x + 8) \rightarrow 3 \cdot 5x = 15x$

LAST $(2x + 3)(5x + 8) \quad 3 \cdot 8 = 24$

TOTAL $10x^2 + 31x + 24$

FOIL is a "shorthand" way to multiply 2 binomials.

97

NEGATIVE NUMBERS

x $\quad$ x $\quad$ -1

$x^2 - x$

$(x+2)(x-1)$

$= x^2 + 2x - x - 2$

$x^2 + x - 2$

$(x-1)(x-1)$

positive

$= x^2 - 2x + 1$

$(2x+1)(x-2)$

$2x^2 + x - 4x - 2$

$2x^2 - 3x - 2$

$$(x-2)(x-3)$$

$\rightarrow x^2 - 5x + 6$

#1

$$(x+2)(x+1)$$

BY THE DISTRIBUTIVE PROPERTY

$$x(x+1) + 2(x+1)$$

$$x^2 + x + 2x + 2$$

$$x^2 + 3x + 2$$

#2

$$(x+2)(x+1)$$

BY FOIL

F O I L
$x^2 + x + 2x + 2$

$x^2 + 3x + 2$

#3 SHOW GEOMETRICALLY

$= x^2 + 3x + 2$

3 SPECIAL EXAMPLES

① $(a+b)^2$ THE SQUARE OF A SUM

$= a^2 + 2ab + b^2$

② $(a-b)^2$ THE SQUARE OF A DIFFERENCE

$= a^2 - 2ab + b^2$

③ $(a+b)(a-b)$ THE PRODUCT OF A SUM AND A DIFFERENCE

$= a^2 - b^2$

PROBLEM

A RECTANGULAR GARDEN IS 10 FT
LONGER THAN WIDE. A BRICK PATH
3 FT. WIDE SURROUNDS THE GARDEN.
THE TOTAL AREA OF THE PATH IS
396 SQ FT. WHAT ARE THE
DIMENSIONS OF THE GARDEN?

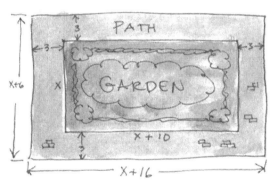

TOTAL AREA − GARDEN AREA = 396

$(x+6)(x+16) - x(x+10) = 396$

$x^2 + 22x + 96 - x^2 - 10x = 396$

$12x + 96 = 396$

$12x = 300$

$x = 25$

THE GARDEN IS
25 FT × 35 FT

FACTO

IS " UNMULTIPLY IN

MULTIPLY		
$2(3)$	$=$	6
$X(X+1)$	$=$	$X^2 + X$
$2X(X+3)$	$=$	$2X^2 +$
$(X+1)(X+2)$	$=$	$X^2 + 3X$
$X(X+2)(X+3)$	$=$	$X^3 + 5X^2$

FACTORING IS THE "HEART"
OF ALGEBRA

)RING

G' LIKE BELOW

FACTOR

$$= \quad 2(3)$$

$$= \quad X(X+1)$$

$$6X = 2X(X+3)$$

$$+2 = (X+1)(X+2)$$

$$+6X = X(X+2)(X+3)$$

THERE ARE SPECIFIC
METHODS OF FACTORING

"SCALE THE CLIFF"
(an analogy for success in algebra)

DARK CLOUDS

LOOKING FOR THE QUICK SOLUTION

THE WRONG DIRECTION

ROCKS OF DISCOURAGE.

FALSE CONCLUSIONS

WORKING TOO FAST

GIVING UP TOO EASILY

WINDING PATH TO THE SOLUTION

SOLUTION

SOLID AND SECURE STEPS ARE THE SURE WAY TO THE TOP

MENT

DISCOURAGEMENT

QUICK SAND OF CARELESSNESS

Greatest Common Factor (GCF)

Look for the factor that all monomials or terms have in common.

What do the 3 figures above have in common? Answer the + sign.

Likewise, what do the 3 numbers below have in common?

$$6 \qquad 21 \qquad 15$$

All 3 have a factor (divisible by) of 3.

We refer to the Greatest Common Factor as the GCF.

Always look to see if there is GCF first before looking for other factors or ways to factor.

Note: Make certain that the common factor is also the greatest (the largest).

For example, 2 is a common factor of

8, 12, and 16

but the <u>greatest</u> common factor is 4.

PRIME FACTORIZATION

FIND THE FACTORS THAT CANNOT
BE FACTORED.

PRIME NUMBERS: NUMBERS WHOSE
ONLY FACTORS ARE ONE AND THEMSELVES.

An example
of
"a factor tree"

The prime factors of 64 are

$2 \cdot 2 \cdot 2 \cdot 2 \cdot 2 \cdot 2$ or 2^6

Likewise, algebraic expressions
can be factored.

108

Use the GCF together with the
distributive property to factor
polynomials.

EXAMPLE 1

$$3X^2 - 8X$$

GCF = X $X(3X) - X(8)$ use
distributive
property

$$X(3X-8)$$

EXAMPLE 2

$$10y^2 + 15y$$

GCF = $5y$ $10y^2 = 2\boxed{5 \cdot y} y$ FACTORS
$15y = 3\boxed{5 \cdot y}$

$$10y^2 + 15y$$

$$5y(2y) + 5y(3)$$

$$5y(2y+3) \quad \text{FACTORS}$$

FACTORING POLYNOMIALS GEOMETRICALLY

$$X^2 - 4X$$

Build a rectangle from the polynomial

the factors are X and $X - 4$

or

$$X(X-4)$$

$$3X^2 - 6X$$

$$= 3X(X-2)$$

THE SIEVE OF ERATOSTHENES

Eratosthenes was a Greek poet and
astronomer (c. 200 B.C.). He is
credited with originating a way
to calculate or "find" prime numbers.

(2) (3) 4̸ (5) 6̸ (7) 8̸ 9̸ 1̸0̸
1̸ 1̸2̸ (13) 1̸4̸ 1̸5̸ 1̸6̸ (17) 1̸8̸ (19)
2̸0̸ 2̸1̸ 2̸2̸ (23) 2̸4̸ 2̸5̸ 2̸6̸ 2̸7̸ 2̸8̸
(29) 3̸0̸ (31) 3̸2̸ 3̸3̸ 3̸4̸ 3̸5̸ 3̸6̸ (37)
3̸8̸ 3̸9̸ 4̸0̸ (41) 4̸2̸ (43) 4̸4̸ 4̸5̸
4̸6̸ (47) 4̸8̸ 4̸9̸ 5̸0̸ - - -

Begining after 2, cross out every 2nd
number.
   After 3, cross out every third number.
   After 4, cross out every fourth number
   After 5, etc - - -

111

the key to factoring is
answering a simple question:
for any given number, what
2 numbers when multiplied
together will produce
the given number?

Unfortunately, a formula
for factoring has never been
devised.

Sometimes you can factor
polynomials by [GROUPING]

EXAMPLE
FACTOR

$$3xy - 21y + 5x - 35$$

$$3y(x-7) + 5(x-7)$$

BY
DIST. $\longrightarrow$ $(3y+5)(x-7)$
PROP.

ANOTHER EXAMPLE

?

? | AREA =
$6x^3 - 10x^2 + 21x - 35$

$$6x^3 - 10x^2 + 21x - 35$$

$$2x^2(3x-5) + 7(3x-5)$$

$$(2x^2+7)(3x-5)$$

$$2x^2+7 \text{ by } 3x-5$$

What is the pattern?

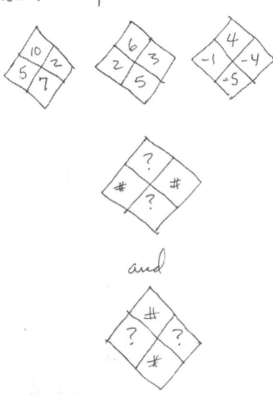

and

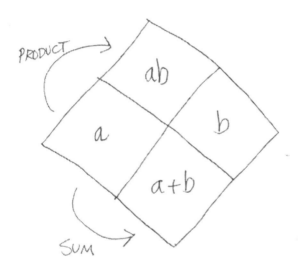

PRODUCT

ab

a

b

a+b

SUM

What 2 numbers are
factors of ab and addends of
a+b?

Factoring Trinomials

(Remember that the product of 2 binomials (by FOIL) is most often a trinomial.)

$$x^2 + 5x + 6$$

↑
FACTOR
1 · 1

↑
FACTOR
6 · 1
2 · 3

ADDED

$$(x+2)(x+3)$$

Check by FOIL

Factoring trinomials can also be done with manipulatives. Example?

116

$$2y^2 + 7y + 6$$

$2 \cdot 1$ $6 \cdot 1$

                $3 \cdot 2$

$(2 \times 3) + (1 \times 2) = 8$ paired incorrectly

$$2y^2 + 7y + 6$$

F $2 \cdot 1$ $6 \cdot 1$

        I $3 \cdot 2$ L

     O

$(2 \times 2) + (1 \times 3) =$ ✓

$(2y + 3)(y + 2)$

The "UN-FOIL" Method

117

$$a^2 - 9a - 36$$

(F) $1 \cdot 1$ (I) $+$ $3 \cdot 12$ (L)

(O) $(-)$

$$(a + 3)(a - 12)$$

$$5x^2 - 17x + 14$$

$14 \cdot 1$

(F) $5 \cdot 1$ (I) $(-)$ $7 \cdot 2$ (L)

(O) $(-)$

$$(5x - 7)(x - 2)$$

pair off the factors
and identify F·O·I·L
components

118

FACTORING THE DIFFERENCE OF SQUARES

$$\boxed{a^2} - \boxed{b^2}$$

$$a^2 - b^2 = (a+b)(a-b)$$

EXAMPLE #1

$$a^2 - 64$$

$$(a)^2 - (8)^2$$

$$(a+8)(a-8)$$

#2

$$9x^2 - 100y^2$$

$$(3x+10y)(3x-10y)$$

The middle term cancels out.

119

ANOTHER WAY TO FACTOR
TRINOMIALS

Step #1 - MULTIPLY 1ST + 3RD TERM COEFFICIENTS

$$X^2 + 5X + 6 \rightarrow 6 \times 1 = 6$$

Step #2 SET UP A FACTOR/ADDEND TABLE   ⑥

×	+
6·1	7
2·3	5 ✓

Step #3 REWRITE MID TERM

$$X^2 + 5X + 6$$
$$X^2 + 2X + 3X + 6$$

Step #4 GROUP

$$(X^2 + 2X) + (3X + 6)$$

Step #5 GCF

$$X(X+2) + 3(X+2)$$

Step #6 FACTOR BY DIST. PROP.

$$(X+3)(X+2)$$

FACTORING A "DIFFICULT" TRINOMIAL

$$4x^2 + 4x - 3$$

$$+6x \quad -2x$$

$$4x^2 + 6x - 2x - 3$$

$$2x(2x+3) - 1(2x+3)$$

$$(2x-1)(2x+3)$$

$\times$	$+$
$12 \cdot 1$	$1 - 12 = -11$
$3 \cdot 4$	$3 - 4 = -1$
$6 \cdot 2$	$4 - 3 = 1$
	$2 - 6 = -4$
	$6 - 2 = 4 \checkmark$

-12

This method works for all factorable trinomials.

Note: Not all trinomials can be factored. EXAMPLE

$$x^2 + x + 3$$

123

FACTORED TRINOMIALS
CAN BE CHECKED
BY FOIL OR BY
THE FOLLOWING METHOD:

The factors of $4x^2 + 4x - 3$
are $(2x - 1)$ and $(2x + 3)$

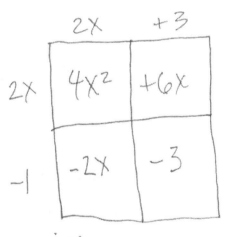

	$2x$	$+3$
$2x$	$4x^2$	$+6x$
-1	$-2x$	-3

yields $4x^2 + 4x - 3$

Checks ✓

PERFECT SQUARES

$$\left(\boxed{a} + \boxed{b} \right)^2$$

OR

$$\left(\boxed{a} - \boxed{b} \right)^2$$

become

$$a^2 + 2ab + b^2$$

and

$$a^2 - 2ab + b^2$$

1. The first term is a square
2. The third term is a square
3. The 2nd term is twice the product of the 1st and 3rd

123

EQUATIONS CAN BE SOLVED BY FACTORING

$$x^2 + 2x = 0$$

$$x(x+2) = 0$$

$x = 0$ $\begin{cases} x+2 = 0 \\ x = -2 \end{cases}$

if the product of 2 numbers equals zero, one or both must equal zero

SOLUTIONS 0 and -2

$$3y^2 + 11y + 10 = 0$$

$$(3y+5)(y+2) = 0$$

$3y+5 = 0$ $\begin{cases} y+2 = 0 \\ y = -2 \end{cases}$
$y = -\frac{5}{3}$

SOLUTIONS $-\frac{5}{3}$ and -2

What number between 2 and 100 has the greatest number of factors?

The "Lost" Factoring Machine

Invented by Eugene Carissan circa 1920. Sat in a desk drawer for decades until recently discovered. Factors up to 13 digit numbers.

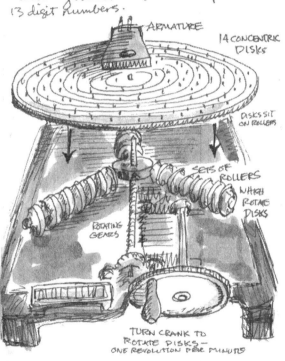

ARMATURE

14 CONCENTRIC DISKS

DISKS SIT ON ROLLERS

SETS OF ROLLERS WHICH ROTATE DISKS

ROTATING GEARS

TURN CRANK TO ROTATE DISKS — ONE REVOLUTION PER MINUTE

Our decimal number
system was introduced
by Leonardo Fibonacci
in 1202
In his book, "Book of Calculating"
It was basically a Hindu-
Arabic number system.

9 8 7 6 5 4 3 2 1 and 0

Zero comes from

In Fibonacci's book he
introduces a problem for his
readers to use to practice
their math –

"A pair of rabbits are put in a
field and, if the rabbits take a
month to become mature and
then produce a new pair every
month after that, how many pairs
will there be in twelve month's time?"

The answer involves the
series of numbers:

1, 1, 2, 3, 5, 8, 13, 21, ...

This series of numbers is called the "Fibonacci Series" and appears throughout nature.

The numbers in the series are called "Fibonacci Numbers"

1, 1, 2, 3, 5, 8, 13, 21, 34, 55, 89, 144, ...

These are the first 12 Fibonacci numbers. You can calculate each number by simply adding the previous 2 numbers. Their sum is the next number.

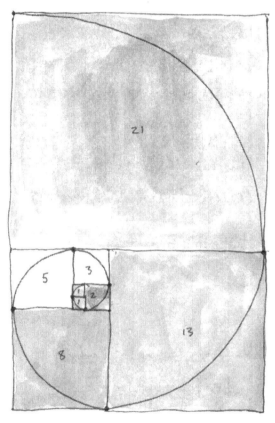

21

3

5

2

8

13

A Fibonacci series as it relates
to geometry. The nautilus shell
is an example in nature.

129

Fractions in Algebra are handled in the same manner as all other fractions. Fractional expressions are called "Rational Expressions".

In the expression $\dfrac{6x}{x+7}$ $x \neq -7$

$$\dfrac{2a-3}{a^2-a-12}$$ FACTOR

$$\dfrac{2a-3}{(a-4)(a+3)}$$ $a \neq 4 \text{ or } -3$

All operations obey the rules for handling fractions.

Express the area of the
rectangle in simplest form

$$2x + 4 = \frac{2(x+2)}{x}$$

$$\frac{x^3 - 4x}{x^2 + 4x + 4} = \frac{x(x^2-4)}{(x+2)^2} = \frac{x(x+2)(x-2)}{}$$

$$A = h \cdot w$$

$$= \frac{2(x+2) \times (x+2)(x-2)}{x \cdot (x+2)(x+2)}$$

$$= 2(x-2)$$

Division is multiplication by reciprocal.
"To divide fractions, don't ask why —
flip the divisor and multiply!"

Where is the fallacy?

given $a = b$

$$a \cdot a = b \cdot a \quad \text{mult. by } a$$

$$a^2 = ab \quad \text{simplify}$$

$$a^2 - b^2 = ab - b^2 \quad \text{sub. } b^2$$

$$\frac{(a-b)(a+b)}{a-b} = \frac{b(a-b)}{a-b} \quad \text{Factor} \quad \text{divide by } (a-b)$$

$$a + b = b$$

$$b + b = b \quad \text{Substitute}$$

$$\frac{2b}{b} = \frac{b}{b} \quad \text{divide by } b$$

$$2 = 1$$

What is wrong?

DIVIDE POLYNOMIALS BY BINOMIALS

EXAMPLE #1

$$\begin{array}{r} x + 3 \\ x+5 \overline{\smash{\big)}\ x^2 + 8x + 15} \\ \underline{-\ x^2 \mp 5x} \\ +3x + 15 \\ \underline{\mp 3x \mp 15} \\ 0 \qquad \text{NO Remainder} \end{array}$$

EXAMPLE #2

$$\begin{array}{r} x - 7 \\ 2x+3 \overline{\smash{\big)}\ 2x^2 - 11x - 20} \\ \underline{-\ 2x^2 \mp 3x} \\ -14x - 20 \\ \underline{\pm 14x \pm 21} \\ +1 \ \text{remainder} \end{array}$$

Thus:

$$\frac{2x^2 - 11x - 20}{2x + 3} = x - 7 + \frac{1}{2x + 3}$$

REMAINDER ↗

133

Complex Expressions and
Complex Fractions

$$\frac{3\frac{1}{2}}{5\frac{2}{3}} \quad \text{or} \quad \frac{\frac{1}{x} + \frac{1}{y}}{\frac{1}{x} - \frac{1}{y}}$$

Handle the numerators
and denominators separately
(simplify each as much as poss.)
Then set up as

$$\frac{\frac{a}{b}}{\frac{c}{d}} = \frac{ad}{bc} \quad \text{because} = \frac{a}{b} \cdot \frac{d}{c}$$

GRAPHING

POINTS ARE CALLED "ORDERED
PAIRS" - each point is named
by its position relative to the
x, y axes.

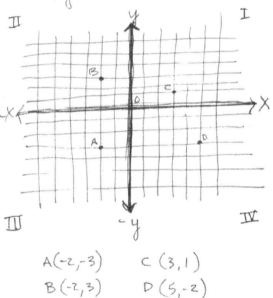

A (-2, -3)   C (3, 1)

B (-2, 3)   D (5, -2)

GIVEN AN EQUATION $3y + 6x = 12$

and the domain is the set $\{-4, -3, -2, 2, 3, 4\}$

The solutions are shown in a table

X	$4 - 2x$	y	(x, y)
-4	$4 - 2(-4)$	12	$(-4, 12)$
-3	$4 - 2(-3)$	10	$(-3, 10)$
-2	$4 - 2(-2)$	8	$(-2, 8)$
2	$4 - 2(2)$	0	$(2, 0)$
3	$4 - 2(3)$	-2	$(3, -2)$
4	$4 - 2(4)$	-4	$(4, -4)$

If the graph is a straight line, it is a linear equation.

Our system for graphing was developed by René Descartes. This coordinate system is called the Cartesian Coordinate System in honor of Descartes.

The connecting of algebra and geometry through graphing is called ANALYTIC GEOMETRY. Descartes was also one of the first to envision the computer. He also believed very strongly in a supreme intelligence or God.

The $\boxed{\text{slope}}$ m of a line is equal
to the change in y divided
by the change in x.

$$\text{SLOPE} = \frac{\text{RISE}}{\text{RUN}} \uparrow \rightarrow$$

Given coordinates $(x_1, y_1)(x_2, y_2)$
the slope is

$$m = \frac{y_2 - y_1}{x_2 - x_1} \quad \text{where } x_2 \neq x_1$$

The $\boxed{\text{POINT - SLOPE}}$ form

$$y - y_2 = m(x - x_2)$$

Which can be derived directly
from the slope formula.

138

The $\boxed{\text{SLOPE - INTERCEPT}}$ form

Given the Y-intercept b and
slope m

$$y = mx + b$$

at the Y-intercept $x = 0$

using

$$y - y_1 = m(x - x_1)$$
$$y - b = mx \qquad \text{derive}$$
$$y = mx + b$$

Given these forms, it is
possible to write equations
from graphs (the reverse of
graphing equations).

SIMULTANEOUS EQUATIONS

A system of equations that has exactly one solution is said to be consistent and independent.

EXAMPLE

$$X - 3y = 6$$
$$X - y = 4$$

One way to solve is by graphing
(the coordinates of the point of intersection)

Another way is by substitution

$$X - 3y = 6$$
$$X - y = 4 \qquad X = y + 4 \quad \text{substitute}$$

$$y + 4 - 3y = 6$$
$$-2y = 2 \quad y = -1$$

then $X - (-1) = 4 \quad X = 3$

A Third method is Elimination
of one of the variables by addition,
subtraction, multiplication.

$$x - 3y = 6$$
$$x - y = 4 \quad \leftarrow \text{subtract}$$

So that

$$\cancel{x} - 3y = 6$$
$$\underline{-\cancel{x} \pm y = -4}$$
$$-2y = 2 \quad y = -1$$

OR

$$x - 3y = 6$$
$$x - y = 4 \quad \longleftarrow \text{mult} -3$$

$$x - 3y = 6$$
$$\underline{-3x + 3y = -12}$$
$$-2x = -6 \quad x = 3$$

An example from the Bible which indicates how math and design are important can be found in the description of the Tabernacle or "the tent of meeting."

The structure, materials, colors, and dimensions are all given. Exodus 35-40.

Bezalel was placed in charge of the workmen and craftsmen. The design shows 2 things: that mathematical precision and also visual beauty are important.

— = THE TABERNACLE IN THE WILDERNESS = —
STRUCTURE & DIMENSIONS

60 Pillars surround the court
supported linen fence 5 cu. high

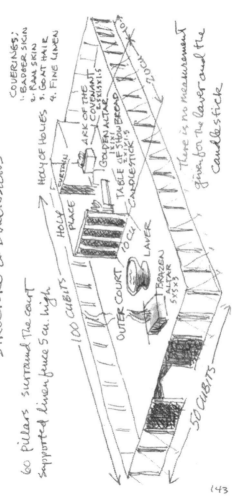

COVERINGS;
1. BADGER SKIN
2. RAM SKIN
3. GOAT HAIR
4. FINE LINEN

ARK OF THE
COVENANT
2.5x1.5x1.5
MERCY

GOLDEN ALTAR
1x1
TABLE of SHOW BREAD
2x1x1.5
CANDLESTICK

HOLY of HOLIES

HOLY
PLACE

10 CU.

LAVER

BRAZEN
ALTAR
5x5x3

OUTER COURT

100 CUBITS

50 CUBITS

20 CU.

10 CU.

There is no measurement
given for the laver and the
Candlestick

143

When the Hebrew people had settled in the promised land, the need for a tabernacle which could be transported from place to place was replaced by the need for a permanent structure.

Solomon built the temple.

In many ways the design of the temple "mirrors" the design of the tabernacle.

Descriptions can be found in I Kings 5-8 and II Chronicles 2-5.

144

בית המקדש

SOLOMON'S TEMPLE

DIMENSIONS
LENGTH = 60 CUBITS
WIDTH = 20 CUBITS
HEIGHT = 30 CUBITS
PORTICO 10 CU. DEEP
SIDE ROOMS, 3 FLRS.
5-7 CUBITS WIDE
5 CUBITS HIGH
INNER SANCTUARY
20 X 20 X 20

145

SPIRALS IN NATURE

There are numerous examples of spirals throughout nature — from the nautilus shell to the ram's horns to the patterns of growth in flowers.

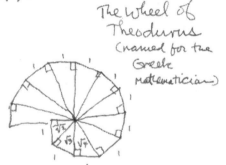

The Wheel of Theodorus (named for the Greek mathematician)

The radii are the hypotenuses of right triangles. Their lengths are $\sqrt{2}$, $\sqrt{3}$, $\sqrt{4}$, $\sqrt{5}$, etc.

The Pythagorean Theorem

In a right triangle, if a
and b are the measures of
the legs and c is the measure
of the hypotenuse, then

$$a^2 + b^2 = c^2$$

or

$$c = \sqrt{a^2 + b^2}$$

Pythagoras
was another
Greek
mathematician

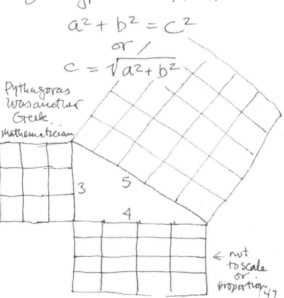

3

5

4

← not
to scale
or
proportion 47

APPLICATION

A car traveling S mph skids d feet after the brakes are applied is represented by the formula $S = \sqrt{30fd}$ where f represents the coefficient of friction.

If the car is traveling 30 mph and skidded on wet pavement 110 ft and the friction = 0.4 for wet concrete, then

$$30 = \sqrt{30(0.4)d}$$

$$30 = \sqrt{12d}$$

$$30^2 = 12d$$

$$d = 75$$

Therefore, the car skidded 75 ft. after the brakes were applied and not 110 ft. as shown by the skid marks.

PHYSICS

time (t) that it takes an object, initially at rest, to fall a distance of s meters is given by the formula $t = \sqrt{\dfrac{2s}{g}}$ where g is the acceleration due to gravity in meters per second.

Problem

On the moon, a rock falls 7.2 meters in 3 seconds.

$$3 = \sqrt{\frac{14.4 \, m}{g}}$$

$$9 = \frac{14.4}{g}$$

$$9g = 14.4$$

$$g = 1.6 \, m/s^2$$

GRAPHING QUADRATIC FUNCTIONS

EXAMPLE

$$y = X^2 - 4X + 1$$

X	$X^2 - 4X + 1$	y
-1	$(-1)^2 - 4(-1) + 1$	6
0	$0^2 - 4(0) + 1$	1
1	$1^2 - 4(1) + 1$	-2
2	$2^2 - 4(2) + 1$	-3
3	$3^2 - 4(3) + 1$	-2
4	$4^2 - 4(4) + 1$	1
5	$5^2 - 4(5) + 1$	6

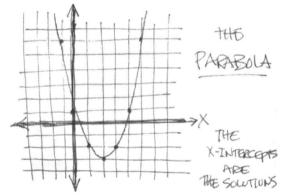

THE
PARABOLA

THE
X-INTERCEPTS
ARE
THE SOLUTIONS

SOLVING QUADRATICS BY COMPLETING THE SQUARE

METHOD: SET UP THE EQUATION SO THAT A PERFECT SQUARE TRINOMIAL EQUALS A CONSTANT

E.G.

$$x^2 + 6x - 16 = 0$$

$+16$	$x^2 + 6x = 16$
$+9$	$x^2 + 6x + 9 = 16 + 9$
EXPRESS AS SQUARE	$(x+3)^2 = 25$
$\sqrt{}$	$x + 3 = \pm 5$
-3	$x = -8, +2$

SOLUTION $x = \{-8, 2\}$

DERIVING THE QUADRATIC FORMULA

THE QUADRATIC FORM

$$ax^2 + bx + c = 0$$

QUADRATIC TERM   LINEAR TERM   CONSTANT

$$ax^2 + bx + c = 0$$

$\div a$

$$x^2 + \frac{b}{a}x + \frac{c}{a} = 0$$

$-\frac{c}{a}$

$$x^2 + \frac{b}{a}x = -\frac{c}{a}$$

COMP SQ.

$$x^2 + \frac{b}{a}x + \left(\frac{b}{2a}\right)^2 = -\frac{c}{a} + \left(\frac{b}{2a}\right)^2$$

FACTOR

$$\left(x + \frac{b}{2a}\right)^2 = -\frac{c}{a} + \frac{b^2}{4a^2}$$

SIMPLY

$$\left(x + \frac{b}{2a}\right)^2 = \frac{b^2 - 4ac}{4a^2}$$

$\sqrt{}$

$$x + \frac{b}{2a} = \pm\sqrt{\frac{b^2 - 4ac}{4a^2}}$$

SIMP $-\frac{b}{2a}$

$$x = \frac{-b \pm \sqrt{b^2 - 4ac}}{2a}$$

3 METHODS FOR SOLVING QUADRATIC EQUATIONS

1. FACTORING

2. COMPLETING THE SQUARE

3. THE QUADRATIC FORMULA

A 4th METHOD IS GRAPHING (least reliable)

These are listed in order of difficulty from simplest solution to the most complex.

153

THE DISCRIMINANT

The expression $b^2 - 4a$ which is the expression under the radical in the quadratic is called the discriminant. The discriminant can tell us many things about the the nature of roots of the equation.

When the discriminant is positive, there are 2 distinct real roots. When the discriminant is zero, there is exactly one distinct root. When the discriminant is negative, there are no real roots.

Analysis of The 4 methods of solving Quadratic equations.

METHOD	CAN BE USED	COMMENTS
GRAPHING	ALWAYS	inexact; use only when an approx. solution is sufficient
FACTORING	SOMETIMES	Use if factors are easily determined
COMPLETING THE SQUARE	ALWAYS	useful for equations where the linear term coefficient is an even numb.
QUADRATIC FORMULA	ALWAYS	Not the easiest, but always accurate

$$w \boxed{\begin{array}{c} \ell \\ A = 221 \end{array}}$$

$\ell + w = 30$ perimeter $= 60$

Set $\ell = x$ $\ell + w = \frac{1}{2} \cdot 60$

then $w = 30 - x$

$$x(30 - x) = 221 \qquad \ell = 13$$
$$30x - x^2 - 221 = 0 \qquad w = 17$$
$$\qquad\qquad\qquad\qquad or$$
$$x^2 - 30x + 221 = 0 \qquad \ell = 17$$
$$(x - 13)(x - 17) = 0 \qquad w = 13$$
$$x = 13, 17$$

155

Further details of Quadratics:
$$ax^2 + bx + c = 0 \quad \text{(standard form)}$$

the sum of the roots $= -\dfrac{b}{a}$

the product of the roots $= \dfrac{c}{a}$

What are the odds that
in a group of 25 people, two
will have the same birthday?

Almost 2 to 1!

Explanation:

For 2 people each would have the odds of
$\frac{1}{365}$

3 peo. each $\frac{2}{365}$ or $3 \cdot \frac{2}{365}$

10 peo each $\frac{9}{365}$ total $= 10 \cdot \frac{9}{365}$

20 peo each $\frac{19}{365}$ TOTAL $= 20 \cdot \frac{19}{365}$

(ABOUT EVEN ODDS)

25 peo. each $\frac{24}{365}$ TOTAL $= 25 \cdot \frac{24}{365}$

or $\frac{600}{365}$!

Charles Lutwidge Dodgson (1832-1898)
aka Lewis Carroll was an English mathematician

In "Through the Looking Glass" the
following problem appears:
"Tweedledum said to Tweedledee : "The
sum of your weight and twice mine
is 361 pounds." Tweedledee said to
Tweedledum : "Contrariwise, the sum of
your weight and twice mine is 362 pounds."

$$x + 2y = 361$$
$$2x + y = 362$$

A CURIOUS FACT

(All rational numbers can be
written as the quotient of two
integers)

Here is an example:
    Divide 7 into any integer
between 1 and 6. Carry it out to
12 decimal places.

    Somewhere in the answer the
sequence 142857 will
        appear!

To The horizon
The distance that can
be seen from an
airborn craft is
calculated using the formula

$$d = \sqrt{\frac{3}{2}h}$$

For a height of 1 mile (5280 ft)

$$d = \sqrt{\frac{3 \cdot 5280}{2}}$$

NOTE

h is measured
in feet and
d = miles

$$= \sqrt{3 \cdot 2640}$$

$$= \sqrt{7920}$$

$$\approx 89 \text{ MILES}$$

Ram's horns
Examples of the

$$\sqrt{1}, \sqrt{2}, \sqrt{3}, \sqrt{4}, \sqrt{5}, \dots \text{ spiral}$$

160

PASCAL'S TRIANGLE

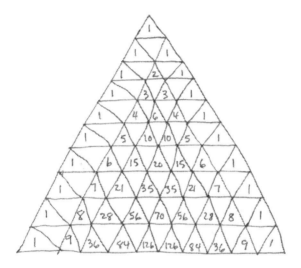

Sequences of numbers

SIERPENSKI'S TRIANGLE

This triangle can be created
2 different ways and
is related to Pascal's triangle.

STATISTICS AND PROBABILITY

The use of algebra to work
with statistics (gathered data)
and probability (the calculation
of mathematical models from
which to predict outcomes) is
a relatively new area of
study. This began to interest
mathematicians in the mid
18th century.

Jacob Bernoulli (1654-1705)
is considered to be the founder
of probability.

SEQUENCES AND MUSIC

BLOCKS OF HARDWOOD

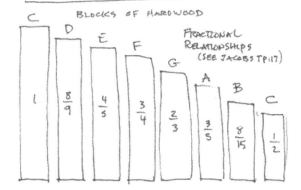

FRACTIONAL RELATIONSHIPS
(SEE JACOBS Tp 117)

C — 1
D — $\frac{8}{9}$
E — $\frac{4}{5}$
F — $\frac{3}{4}$
G — $\frac{2}{3}$
A — $\frac{3}{5}$
B — $\frac{8}{15}$
C — $\frac{1}{2}$

THE MUSICAL SCALE

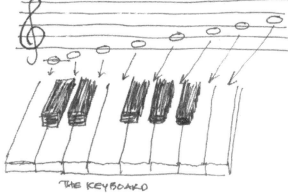

THE KEYBOARD

NOTES / STEPS

SEQUENCES AND COLOR

Color is the visible part of the
electro-magnetic (Radiant energy)
scale.

Speed of light ≈ 186,000 miles per second

| ELEC. POWER | INDUCTIVE HEAT | RADIO/TV | INFRA RED | | UV | X-RAY | GAMMA RAYS | COSMIC RAYS |

THE
VISIBLE
SPECTRUM

| 7500λ | 7000 RED | 6500 ORANGE | 6000 YELLOW | 5500 GREEN | 4500 BLUE | 4000 VIOLET |

λ - angstrom units measure wavelength
Frequency times wavelength = speed of light

Music and color have often

been compared for their harmonies,
contrasts, variations, etc.

165

π · MAY I HAVE A LARGE CONTAINER OF COFFEE
3 1 4 1 5 9 2 6

(pi) is perhaps the most important mathematical concept that we have. π is the relationship between the diameter of a circle and the circumference $(C = \pi \cdot D)$. It defines many other relationships.

π is an irrational number. It has been calculated to more than a million decimal places.

Most often we use $\frac{22}{7}$ or 3.14

Although the Greeks knew of the number, it wasn't until the 18th century that the number became identified with the name and symbol. The number is mentioned in the Bible in I Kings 7:23.

166

FACTORING

In the 17th century the following number

1376861049398972053177760857550
6090561429353935989033525802
891469459697

was proposed prime by the French mathematician Marin Mersenne. It has been called Mersenne's Number. In 1984 a Cray computer found that there were 3 factors for this number. The factors are

178230287214063289511 and
61676882198695257501367 and
1207039617824989303996681

This is significant because cryptographic systems depend upon multidigit numbers. Factors provide an easier access to the secure information.

This famous puzzle by Sam Loyd is an excellent example of how algebra makes complicated problems easy to solve.

How many glasses will it take to balance the bottle?

How to Solve using algebra

Let B = bottle, G = glass, S = saucer, and P = pitcher

Then translate the illustrations into the following equations:

#1 $B + G = P$

#2 $B = G + S$

#3 $2P = 3S$

#4 $B = ?$

If $B + G = P$ (#1) Then $P = B + G$ (reflexive)
  Substitute for P in #3 and solve for S
  $2(B+G) = 3S$ then $S = \frac{2}{3}(B+G)$

Substitute in #2
  $B = G + \frac{2}{3}(B+G)$

$\times 3$ | $3B = 3G + 2(B+G)$
Simp | $3B = 3G + 2B + 2G$
$-2B$ | $B = 3G + 2G$
Combine | $B = 5G$

5 glasses is the answer.
Simple!

169

A SIMPLE, BASIC PROGRAM FOR FINDING FACTORS AND IDENTIFYING PRIME NUMBERS

```
P = 999 : REM SET FOR PRIME
PRINT "WHAT IS THE NUMBER";
INPUT N : REM INPUT NUMBER

PRINT "FACTORS OF"; N; ":"
FOR X = 2 TO N-1 : REM SIEVE LOOP
IF N/X = INT(N/X) THEN PRINT X; : P=0
NEXT X

IF P = 999 THEN PRINT "PRIME"
```

RUN THIS PROGRAM AND SEE
IF 4000001 CAN BE FACTORED
OR IS A PRIME NUMBER.

AN INTRIGUING TOPIC

LINEAR EQUATIONS ARE
1-DIMENSIONAL WHEN GRAPHED.
THEY RELATE TO ONE DIMENSION IN REALITY
QUADRATICS ARE **2**-DIMENSIONAL

THEY CAN BE USED TO DESCRIBE

2-DIMENSIONAL OBJECTS IN

REALITY.

AN EXPONENT OF 3 (THE THIRD

POWER) RELATES TO THE 3-D WORLD.

IN ALGEBRA IT IS POSSIBLE TO EXPRESS
DIMENSIONS HIGHER THAN 3. A
4-DIMENSIONAL FIGURE HAS BEEN
NAMED. IT IS CALLED A TESSERACT.

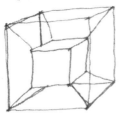

Are there
really more
than 4 dimensions?
There are in theory.

THE TESSERACT

π REVISITED

3.14159265358979
3238462643383279
5028841971693993
7510582097494459
2307816406286208
9986280348253421
1706798214808651
32823066...

- Endless
- non-repeating
- irrational

```
              A
            A   L   A
          A   L   G   L   A
        A   L   G   E   G   L   A
      A   L   G   E   B   E   G   L   A
    A   L   G   E   B   R   B   E   G   L   A
  A   L   G   E   B   R   A   R   B   E   G   L   A
```

How many different ways can the word algebra be spelled?

There are 7 letters in the word and thus 7 rows.

The total can be expressed in the formula $T = 2^R - 1$

where R = the row

In this example $T = 2^7 - 1 = 127$

SOME DEFINITIONS

Absolute Value - The absolute value of a number is the number of units that it is from zero on the number line.

Addition property for inequalities

for all numbers a, b, and c,

1. if $a > b$, then $a + c > b + c$ and
2. if $a < b$, then $a + c < b + c$

Addition property of equality

for any numbers a, b, $+ c$,

if $a = b$ then $a + c = b + c$

174

Additive identity

The number 0 (zero) is the additive identity since the sum of any number and zero is equal to the number.

Additive Inverse

Two numbers are additive inverses if their sum is zero. The additive inverse of a is $-a$

Algebraic Expression

An expression consisting of one or more numbers and variables along with one or more arithmetic operations.

Associative property of addition

For any numbers a, b, and c

$$(a + b) + c = a + (b + c)$$

Descriptions of materials and the dimensions.

In Revelation 21
there is an amazing
description of the
New Jerusalem
descending from
the heavens

TH

HIGHEST

OF

IS THE SEE

KNOW

O

OUR GOD AN

E

ALGEBRA

ALL

KING AFTER

LEDGE

F

ID CREATOR

"Math is the language God used to create the universe." — GOETHE

MORE DEFINITIONS

[B] __Base__ in an expression of the form X^n, the base is X.

__Binomial__ A polynomial with exactly 2 terms.

__box-and-whisker plot__. In a box and whisker plot, the quartiles and extreme value of a set of data are displayed using a number line.

C Closed half plane - A half plane that includes the boundary.

Coefficient The numerical part of a term.

Commutative property of addition
for any numbers a and b
$$a + b = b + a$$

Commutative property of multiplication
for any numbers a and b, $ab = ba$

Comparison property for rational numbers
for any rational numbers $\frac{a}{b}$ and $\frac{c}{d}$ with
$b > 0$ and $d > 0$
1. if $\frac{a}{b} < \frac{c}{d}$ the $ad < bc$ and
   2. if $ad < bc$ then $\frac{a}{b} < \frac{c}{d}$.

Complementary angles

2

Angles whose sum measures $90°$

Completeness property for points in the plane

when plotting points, the following is true

1. Exactly one point in the plane is named by a given ordered pair of numbers.

2. Exactly one ordered pair of numbers names a given point in the plane.

Completing the square

a method of solving a quadratic equation where a perfect square trinomial is formed on one side of the equation.

Complex fraction — a fraction that has one or more fractions in the numerator or denominator.

$\dfrac{\frac{1}{2}}{\frac{5}{6}}$ is a complex fraction

Composite number — Any positive integer except 1 that is not prime.

Compound event — a compound event consists of 2 or more simple events.

Compound inequalities — Two inequalities connected by and or or.

Compound interest

The amount of interest paid or earned on the original principal plus the accumulated interest.

Conjugates

Two binomials of the form $a\sqrt{b} + c\sqrt{d}$ and $a\sqrt{b} - c\sqrt{d}$

Consecutive even integers

Numbers given when beginning with an even integer and counting by two's.

Consecutive numbers

numbers in counting order.

184

Consecutive odd integers

Numbers given when beginning with an odd integer and counting by twos.

Consistent

a system of equations is consistent and independent if it has one ordered pair as its solution. A system of equations is consistent and dependent if it has infinitely many ordered pairs as its solution.

Constant

A monomial that does not contain variables.

Constant of variation

in the direct variation $y = kx$, k is called the constant of variation.

coordinate   The coordinate
of a point is the number that
corresponds to it on the
number line.

coordinate plane   The
number plane formed by
two perpendicular number
lines that intersect at their
zero points.

cosine   in a right triangle
the cosine (cos) of angle A =

$$\frac{\text{measure of side adjacent to} \angle A}{\text{measure of the hypotenuse}}$$

SOH - CAH - TOA

adj/hypotenuse

D

Data numerical information

Decimal notation A way of expressing numbers using a base ten system.

Degree The degree of a monomial is the sum of the exponents of the variables. The degree of a non-zero constant is 0. The degree of a polynomial is the greatest of the degrees of its terms

Density property
Between every pair of distinct rational numbers, there is another rational number.

Difference of squares

Two perfect squares separated by a subtraction sign.

$$a^2 - b^2$$

Direct Variation

A direct variation is described by an equation of the form $y = kx$, where $k \neq 0$

Discriminant

In the quadratic formula, the expression $b^2 - 4ac$ is called the discriminant.

Disjoint Set

2 sets that have no members in common.

Disjunction A compound sentence where the statements are connected using **or**.

Distance Formula The distance between any 2 points (x_1, y_1) and (x_2, y_2) is given by the formula

$$d = \sqrt{(x_2 - x_1)^2 + (y_2 - y_1)^2}$$

Distributive Property for any numbers a, b, and c:

1. $a(b+c) = ab + ac$ and
   $(b+c)a = ba + ca$

2. $a(b-c) = ab - ac$ and
   $(b-c)a = ba - ca$

Division property for inequalities

For all numbers a, b, and c with $c \neq 0$

1. If c is positive and $a < b$ then $\frac{a}{c} < \frac{b}{c}$
   and if c is positive and $a > b$ then
   $\frac{a}{c} > \frac{b}{c}$

2. If c is negative and $a < b$, then $\frac{a}{c} > \frac{b}{c}$
   and if c is negative and $a > b$ then
   $\frac{a}{c} < \frac{b}{c}$

Division property of Equality

For any numbers a, b, and c
with $c \neq 0$, if $a = b$, then
$$\frac{a}{c} = \frac{b}{c}$$

<u>Domain</u> The domain of a rela-
tion is the set of all first components
from each ordered pair.

$$\boxed{E}$$

<u>Element</u> One of the members of
a set.

<u>Elimination Method</u> A method
for solving systems of equations in
which the equations are added
or subtracted to eliminate one
of the variables. Multiplication
of one or both equations may occur
before the equations are added
or subtracted.

Empty Set a set with no elements.

Equals Sign The equals sign, $=$, between two expressions indicates that if the sentence is true, the expressions name the same number.

Equation A mathematical sentence that contains the equals sign.

Equivalent equations Equations that have the same solution.

<u>Exponent</u> A number used to tell how many times a number is used as a factor. In an expression X^n, The exponent is $\underline{n}$.

F

<u>Factor</u> In a multiplication expression, the quantities being multiplied.

<u>FOIL</u> method for multiplying binomials

To multiply 2 binomials, find The sum of The products of

F The first terms,
O The outer terms.
I The inner terms, and
L the last terms.

<u>Formula</u> - An equation that states a rule for the relationship between certain quantities.

<u>Function</u> - A function is a relation in which each element of the domain is paired with exactly one element of the range.

<u>Functional notation</u> - the functional notation of the equation
$$y = x + 5 \text{ is}$$
$$f(x) = x + 5$$

<u>Functional value</u>

The symbol $f(3)$ represents the functional value of f for $x = 3$.

194

G

Greatest Common Factor (GCF)

The GCF of 2 or more integers is the greatest factor that is common to each of the integers.

Grouping Symbols

Symbols used to clarify or change the order of operations in an expression. Parentheses, brackets, and the fraction bar are grouping symbols.

H

Half-plane

The region of a graph on one side of a boundary.

Identity An equation that is true for every value of the variable.

Inconsistent A system of equations is inconsistent if it has no solution.

Intercept - A point where a graph crosses the x-axis or y-axis.

Irrational numbers - numbers that cannot be expressed in the form $\frac{a}{b}$ where a and b are integers and $b \neq 0$.

L

Like terms terms that contain the same variables, with corresponding variables raised to the same power.

Linear equation an equation that may be written in the form $Ax + By = C$ where A, B, and C are any numbers and A and B are not both 0.

M

Mixed Expression Algebraic expression containing monomials and rational expressions.

N

negative number A number that is graphed on the negative side of the number line.

Number Theory The study of numbers.

O

Odds the ratio of the number of ways the event can occur (success) to the number of ways it cannot occur.

Open Sentence

A sentence containing a symbol to be replaced in order to determine if the sentence is true or false.

Order of operations

1. Simplify the expressions inside grouping symbols.
2. Evaluate all powers
3. Do all multiplication and division from left to right.
4. Then do all additions and subtractions from left to right.

P

Parabola the general shape of the graph of a quadratic function.

Power

An expression of the form x^n

Prime number An integer greater than 1, whose only positive factors are 1 and itself.

Prime Polynomial

A polynomial that cannot
be written as a product
of two or more polynomials.

Probability

The ratio that tells how
likely it is that an event
will take place.

Product property of square roots

for any numbers a and b
where $a \geq 0$ and $b \geq 0$

$$\sqrt{ab} = \sqrt{a} \cdot \sqrt{b}$$

Q

Quadratic formula

for $ax^2 + bx + c = 0$
where $a \neq 0$

$$x = \frac{-b \pm \sqrt{b^2 - 4ac}}{2a}$$

R Radical Equations

equations containing radicals with variables in the radicand.

Range

The range of a relation is the set of all second components from each ordered pair.

Ratio

A comparison of two numbers by division. The ratio of a to b is $\dfrac{a}{b}$

Rationalizing the Denominator

A method used to eliminate radicals from the denominator of a fraction.

Reciprocal

The reciprocal of a number is its multiplicative inverse.

5

Scientific Notation

The form $a \times 10^n$ where $1 \leq a < 10$ and n is an integer.

Simplest form

An expression is in its simplest form if it has no like terms and no parentheses.

Slope

$$\text{Slope} = \frac{\text{Change in } Y}{\text{Change in } X} = \frac{\text{rise}}{\text{run}}$$

T

Trinomial

A polynomial having exactly 3 terms.

U

Uniform Motion

Constant speed or rate

V

Variable

a symbol used to represent an unknown quantity.

For more information about Integer Jim's exciting math adventures, be sure to visit _mathsquad.com_.

24971556R00114

Made in the USA
Lexington, KY
07 August 2013